NATURAL
NEW ZEALAND

SHAUN BARNETT

CRAIG
POTTON
PUBLISHING

Korokoro Stream, Te Urewera National Park

INTRODUCTION

New Zealand is unlike any other place on earth. Straddling latitudes that stretch from subtropical to subantarctic, New Zealand's archipelago supports an extraordinary range of ecosystems. Aside from deserts, tropical rainforest and arctic tundra, most major ecosystems are represented in one form or another. In addition, New Zealand's long isolation from other landmasses enabled the evolution of some improbable creatures.

New Zealand has long been home to several biological 'refugees' including the ancient tuatara, unusual frogs that don't croak, giant land snails and majestic podocarp forests. Many of these life forms survived here long after others of their kind disappeared from the rest of the world. Yet others, like the kiwi and moa, evolved into unique creatures in New Zealand.

Visitors to New Zealand are very soon impressed with the range of landforms and the diversity of natural ecosystems. From the intricate island-studded coastlines of Northland and Coromandel and the classic symmetrical volcanoes of the central North Island, to the heavily glaciated Southern Alps and the sombre southern fiords, this small country possesses a variety of landforms matched by few other places on the planet.

Much of this diversity is protected in a large network of conservation land including some fourteen national parks and nineteen forest parks, as well as numerous scenic and nature reserves. One government body, the Department of Conservation (DoC), is charged with managing these lands, which together comprise some eight million hectares, or nearly one-third of New Zealand's entire land area.

Also on this conservation estate are thousands of kilometres of tracks, with New Zealand boasting one of the largest hut networks anywhere. Tramping, as hiking or bush walking is called in New Zealand, is world renowned and includes Fiordland's Milford and Routeburn Tracks. While these tracks are now so popular they require booking, those seeking solitude can always find it in vast areas of the country, particularly the dense forests of the North Island's interior, and the more remote valleys of the Southern Alps and Fiordland.

This book is intended to celebrate New Zealand's natural places and its native flora and fauna. It is hoped this introductory essay conveys some brief explanations of what makes New Zealand unique, and also gives readers an overview and history of the superb parks and reserves system that exists here.

Much of New Zealand is still utterly wild, but the sheer ruggedness of the landscapes belies a very fragile nature. Humans have had grave impacts on New Zealand and some of this history makes tragic reading. More recently however, some brilliant and innovative conservation efforts have given welcome hope for the future.

Tongariro became New Zealand's first national park (and the world's fourth), when in 1887 Ngati Tuwharetoa's chief Te Heuheu Tukino IV (Horonuku) gifted the volcanoes of the central North Island to the people of New Zealand. In this remarkable act, chief Te Heuheu sought to forever protect the mana (prestige) of his people's sacred mountains (Ruapehu, Ngauruhoe and Tongariro) from exploitation.

New Zealand's second national park, Egmont National Park (established in 1900), was also formed around a volcano – lonely Mt Taranaki. With the exception of the coastal Abel Tasman National Park (1942), the parks created in the first seven decades of the twentieth century were largely centred on scenic mountains. Most of these came in a rash of park formation during the 1950s and '60s and included Fiordland (1952); Aoraki/Mount Cook (1953), Te Urewera (1954), Nelson Lakes (1956), Westland/Tai Poutini (1960), and Mount Aspiring (1964) National Parks.

In the 1980s conservationists began to push for parks in those natural areas that had often before been neglected – lowland forests, wetlands and coastal environments. No longer was scenic grandeur to be the most important consideration with ecological and geological diversity driving park formation as well. Whanganui and Paparoa National Parks, both formed in the mid 1980s, contained important lowland forests, while Kahurangi National Park (1996) has diverse biological and geological values. Most recently, Stewart Island's wild coastlines and lowland forests were recommended for national park status and now form Rakiura National Park – New Zealand's fourteenth.

New Zealand's twenty forest parks were formed as a sister system to the national parks by one of DoC's predecessors, the New Zealand Forest Service. Tararua Forest Park was the first formed in 1954. Others followed, including Kaimanawa, Pureora and Whirinaki Forest Parks.

Establishing parks has meant significant and important progress for conservation in New Zealand. However, doing so has in many ways merely defined the major battlegrounds. The boundaries of a national park may protect an area from mining or timber extraction, but mean nothing to introduced pests and weeds. Brought to New Zealand largely by European settlers, these new forms of life have devastated much of the native flora and fauna, which from long geographic isolation was too evolutionarily naive to cope with the often aggressive imports.

New Zealand may have one of the best records of setting aside conservation lands, but tragically, has one of the worst records of extinctions. Today the Department of Conservation and other conservation groups are fighting to reverse the decline of indigenous species. But it is proving a long and expensive battle. Several species, including the kakapo (the world's only flightless parrot), the takahe (a large flightless rail), and the newly described orange-fronted parakeet, hang on the brink of extinction. Others, even our national icon the kiwi, are threatened too.

The main cause of these species' decline is predation from introduced mammal predators, particularly the stoat, ship rat and possum, and the destruction of native forests by introduced herbivores such as deer and the aforementioned possum. Somewhat paradoxically, conservation in New Zealand is often a matter of killing these pests. While this may seem abhorrent to many visitors, the choice is clear: survival of our most unique flora and fauna can only come at the cost of killing introduced mammals. The reasons for this go back over 100 million years.

Prior to the arrival of Maori in New Zealand around 1000 years ago, New Zealand had been isolated for some 65-80 million years after it broke from the ancient super-continent of Gondwana. Crucially, New Zealand's departure from Gondwana occurred at an important time in the evolution of life on earth. Gondwana, which comprised landmasses now known as India, Africa, Antarctica, Australia, South America and New Zealand, began to break apart some 120 million years ago, just as the first flowering plants were evolving. Of the large fauna, reptiles were then dominant with the first birds starting to evolve.

Critically, the first mammals were only just appearing when New Zealand split off. If any were present on the raft of New Zealand as it began its journey eastwards, they soon died out. Instead, New Zealand was destined to become a land virtually devoid of mammals, enabling birds and other creatures to begin on some unusual evolutionary paths. Many of the ancient plants that dominated Gondwana, including the podocarps and southern beeches, survived as well.

Today some of New Zealand's most distinctive forms of flora clearly have Gondwanan origins: the majestic kauri – trees of incredible girth; giant tree ferns – the largest of which can reach 20 metres in height; and the stately podocarps – distinctive conifers which include New Zealand's tallest tree, the kahikatea. Southern beeches of the genus *Nothofagus* dominate many eastern forests and also large parts of Fiordland and Nelson. These early flowering plants evolved not long before Gondwana split and still occur in South America, New Caledonia, Australia and Papua New Guinea as well as New Zealand.

If the flora of New Zealand is interesting, the fauna proves bizarre. An ancient group of flightless birds known as ratites had evolved before Gondwana split up, and in New Zealand these became the kiwi and moa. At one time there were some twelve species of moa, the largest of which reached two metres in height and weighed over 200 kilograms. Kiwi, while of a less impressive size, are interesting because of their nocturnal habits and keen sense of smell. Other birds including the kakapo, weka and takahe, which arrived here on the wing after the break-up of Gondwana, often evolved to become flightless too. Some, like the ancient wattlebirds – the kokako, saddleback and huia – while not abandoning flight fully, tended to become poor fliers. This is not to say that flightlessness prevailed. Some of New Zealand's avian predators, while of extraordinary size, were deadly on the wing. *Harpogornis*, the world's largest eagle, boasted a three metre wingspan and talons the size of tiger claws. It preyed on moa

and was capable of killing even the largest of them.

Strange too are other groups of endemic animals, which often tended towards gigantism. Giant weta occupied a niche in New Zealand that is occupied elsewhere in the world by mice, while the largest gecko ever known, the 620mm long kawekaweau, also once called New Zealand home.

It would be a mistake however, to think of New Zealand as totally devoid of mammals – those that could swim or fly did arrive. Of three species of native bat, two are still extant, and a number of seals, dolphins and whales also frequent New Zealand's shores. But, by and large, New Zealand's flora and fauna was – when it came to terrestrial mammals – naive.

The arrival of Maori from Polynesia heralded a huge shock to natural New Zealand, or Aotearoa, as the immigrants called the new land. Maori brought with them dogs, and Polynesian rats, or kiore. Kiore quickly devastated many native reptiles and birds, several of which are now present only on offshore islands. Tuatara, a unique reptile thought to have a lineage some 220 million years old, did not co-exist at all well with the rats either.

With the aid of their dogs, Maori became proficient hunters. By around 300-500 years ago the last of the moa had fallen. With them died the giant eagle *Harpogornis*, and other creatures such as the adzebills and New Zealand goose became extinct as well. Maori also devastated many areas with fire. New Zealand's forest area, thought to have covered 85 per cent of the country prior to Maori arrival, was soon reduced to 55 per cent under the impact of their flame.

However, if the impact of Maori was tragic, much worse was to follow when European colonisation began about 1790. The first to arrive were itinerant sealers, who clubbed New Zealand fur seals to within a few blows of extinction. Whales became their next target, but by the mid 1800s both these industries were in decline, largely as a result of their own brutal efficiency. Ship rats, more aggressive than kiore, hitchhiked to New Zealand aboard the sealers' vessels and soon ran ashore. The sealers also released goats and pigs.

The first European missionaries arrived in New Zealand around 1814, and by the late 1830s settlers were arriving in shiploads mainly from the British Isles, but also from Scandinavia, France and Germany. Settlers, hungry for farmland, soon began forest clearance on an unprecedented scale. Although some trees, particularly kauri, were used for timber, in many areas fire was the tool preferred for clearance and colossal wastage ensued. While habitat clearance had a devastating impact on natural New Zealand, it was introduced pests that would most threaten the remaining wildlands.

Scottish red deer were liberated into New Zealand forests in the late 1800s and Australian brush-tailed possums soon followed. Many indigenous plant species were not adapted for browsing by mammals. Consequently, populations of the new pests exploded and threatened to destroy much of the more vulnerable forests.

Three mustelids – stoats, weasels and ferrets – were brought in to control what had become a rabbit plague in the late 1800s. But these efficient killers soon found native birds much easier targets than rabbits. Much later it was found that possums, once thought to be strictly herbivorous, were also raiding native bird nests. Predictably, many of the more vulnerable native animals became extinct (over half the bird species found here prior to Maori arrival are now gone), while others became relegated to pest-free islands.

Over recent decades a large amount of conservation effort has gone into islands. Fortunately, New Zealand has over 600 offshore islands, many of them quite large. As early as 1891, islands were being set aside for nature reserves. The recent history of one island, Kapiti, off Wellington's west coast, reads as an astonishing transformation from a pest-ridden place into a flourishing sanctuary for native flora and fauna. In 1897, when Kapiti Island first became a nature reserve, the island's forests were largely gone and what remained was overrun with wild goats, cats, possums and rats. Early hunting efforts eradicated goats and cats, but it was not until 1980 that a determined effort was made to exterminate possums. It took a dedicated team six years, but it finally succeeded and Kapiti's forests soon flourished.

By the early 1990s, DoC had developed sophisticated techniques for eradicating rats from islands, but nothing the size of Kapiti had then been attempted. In 1996, using helicopters to distribute rat bait from monsoon buckets, the department successfully destroyed every rat – a world first for an island of that size. Birds and reptiles, many of them rare on the mainland, are now thriving on Kapiti, providing glimpses of New Zealand as it was before European arrival.

While DoC's work on islands remains crucial, the department has recognised that they do not provide the full answer. Firstly, the number of islands is limited; secondly, there are many habitats not well represented on islands; and lastly their isolation often restricts public involvement.

What if the techniques for pest control developed on offshore islands were applied to mainland areas? In the mid 1990s DoC began a series of ambitious restoration projects, called 'mainland islands', in several key North and South Island locations. One of these, in Nelson Lakes National Park, aims to restore a beech forest ecosystem around the shores of Lake Rotoiti. Possums, stoats, introduced wasps and rats have all been targeted for control to near-zero levels, and the breeding success of birds like kaka and robins has consequently improved dramatically.

There are now plans to extend the area of the project and to re-introduce lost species like kiwi and yellowhead to the park. Best of all, the park is very accessible to locals and visitors alike, who can now appreciate a magnificent dawn chorus not dissimilar to that of prehistoric times. Such innovative projects give an immense sense of hope for the future of natural New Zealand.

The diversity of New Zealand's wild places can be overwhelming, and visitors with only a short time here have to choose carefully. For those with ornithological inclinations, visits to Wellington's Kapiti Island or Auckland's Tiritiri Matangi Island are a must. Stewart Island provides visitors with the greatest chance of seeing a wild kiwi, while penguins are best observed on the Otago coastline at reserves near Oamaru and Dunedin. Kaikoura's sea-life is famed, offering many opportunities to see whales, dolphins, fur seals or albatrosses.

Trampers have literally hundreds of tracks to choose from, including a range of difficulties to suit all tastes and abilities. Many opt to walk some, or even all of the Great Walks, which include the famous Routeburn and Milford tracks and the Tongariro Circuit. For wild coastlines, trampers need look no further than Kahurangi's Heaphy Track, Stewart Island's North-West Circuit, or the Hollyford Track in Fiordland National Park. Yet others who prefer less-frequented tracks can enjoy Fiordland's marvellously muddy Dusky Track, or Mount Aspiring National Park's trans-alpine Wilkin-Matukituki traverse. While national parks are undoubtedly the focus for many visitors, there is tramping aplenty in the country's forest parks too.

Climbers will find much to impress them, at least on snow and ice. For a basic introduction to New Zealand peaks, the volcanic summits of Taranaki and Tongariro National Park have plenty to offer. Aoraki/Mount Cook National Park remains a mecca for serious alpinists, as is adjacent Westland/ Tai Poutini National Park. Both parks also make superb ski-touring destinations. Inland from Wanaka, Mt Aspiring – the 'Matterhorn' of New Zealand – offers some classic routes, and there are thousands of lesser-known but equally worthy peaks in the remoter parts of the Southern Alps.

New Zealand rock is notorious for its instability. Exceptions are the hard granite and diorite of Fiordland's Darran Mountains, where serious rock climbers can find long and difficult routes. There are also numerous crags around the country providing good climbs, even though these are often shorter routes. Some of the most accessible are the volcanic dykes of Banks Peninsula, near Christchurch.

Although relatively new in New Zealand, sea kayaking is now well established in places like the Bay of Islands, Abel Tasman National Park and the Marlborough Sounds. In Fiordland, Milford and Doubtful Sounds sea kayaking is becoming increasingly popular, and remoter fiords like Dusky Sound offer truly wilderness-style paddling.

A word of caution: visitors to New Zealand are often unprepared for the intensity of the highly changeable maritime weather. Storms can arrive in a matter of hours, and in many mountainous areas rain or snow can fall at any time of year. Some parts of New Zealand are among the wettest places on earth with one year an astonishing fourteen metres of rain falling in one West Coast catchment. Rain however, is an integral part of New Zealand's wild places and if your trip is wet, take solace from the fact that lush rainforests inevitably require a fair amount of rain. Experiencing Milford Sound in a Fiordland downpour may obscure Mitre Peak, but the numerous and bountiful waterfalls will provide ample compensation.

The images that follow capture a variety of New Zealand's natural landscapes in some of its changing moods, as well as a selection of its unique wildlife. They are intended as a brief introduction to the wildlife and wild places of an astonishing country.

Shaun Barnett

Lake Matheson, Westland/Tai Poutini National Park. New Zealand's two highest peaks, Mt Tasman (3497m) and Aoraki/Mt Cook (3754m) are only 30km from the Tasman Sea and rear over the South Island's West Coast. Diverse ecosystems straddle this narrow stretch of land, ranging from coastal and wetland, to montane forest and alpine.

Blue duck (*Hymenolaimus malacorhynchos*), Otoko River, West Coast. Also known by their Maori name whio, which describes the male's shrill whistle, these endemic birds are one of only four torrent ducks in the world.

The West Coast boasts some of the country's most impressive gorges, like this schist gorge in the Whataroa River. The turquoise colour of the water occurs because of fine rock flour, ground by the glaciers at the river's headwaters. These suspended particles refract light in a way that produces the intense colour.

The glacier terminus of the Fox Glacier, in Westland/Tai Poutini National Park. Worldwide, the occurrence of glaciers beside temperate rainforest is a rarity – occurring only in South America and New Zealand. Both the Fox (15 km long) and Franz Josef Glaciers (13 km long) can move at remarkable rates, and were recorded advancing at speeds of up to three to four metres per day during the mid 1990s. However, such bursts of forward activity are now rare, and the glaciers are generally in recession. (Photo: Rob Brown/Hedgehog House)

Late evening light over the upper Fox Glacier névé, Westland/Tai Poutini National Park. The barrier formed by the Southern Alps intercepts vast quantities of moisture from the predominantly westerly weather system, which often falls as snow on the upper peaks. Accumulation of this snow has formed immense snowfields, from which the Fox and Franz Josef Glaciers flow steeply down toward the sea.

The world's only alpine parrot, kea (*Nestor notabilis*) inhabits mountain areas of the South Island. Inquisitive and cheeky, the birds will quite happily destroy trampers' tents and boots, and at road ends even attack cars. This curiosity is part of the kea's remarkable ability to learn about their environment, and recent studies have found their intelligence to be equal with some primates.

The West Coast's Pancake Rocks at Punakaiki are amongst the most distinctive land formations in New Zealand. Sea erosion has created blowholes in the limestone rock, giving spectators impressive displays when a high tide combines with a big sea. (Photo below: Darryn Pegram/ Black Robin Photography)

Endemic to New Zealand, and found only in Fiordland, the West Coast and Stewart Island, Fiordland crested penguins (*Eudyptes pachyrhynchus*) are the world's rarest penguin.

Kahikatea forest crowds over the shores of Bruce Bay, South Westland. Bruce Bay lies at the southern end of the so-called 'beech gap', a large chunk of central and southern Westland where no beech forest occurs. Some theories suggest that severe glaciation in the last ice age wiped out the beech forest, which – due to the very slow dispersal of its seeds - has not yet had sufficient time to recolonise. In the mean time the faster-spreading podocarp and rata/kamahi forests hold dominance. (Photo: Andris Apse)

Pororari River, Paparoa National Park. Another example of Paparoa limestone, the Pororari is typical of several gorged rivers along this section of the West Coast. A walk up the Pororari links with the Inland Pack Track, the most popular overnight trip in the park.

Lake Paringa, South Westland. The West Coast is one of the most important places for wetlands in New Zealand. Many wetlands in other parts of the country have been drained, with the resulting loss of some of our most diverse ecosystems. Here, flax and cabbage trees dominate a succession of vegetation extending back into drier ground. (Photo: Darryn Pegram/Black Robin Photography)

Ivory Lake, West Coast. A remote and little visited place at the head of the Waitaha Valley, the Ivory Glacier is an example of the severe glacial recession that has occurred in New Zealand over the past century. Small glaciers like this one will most likely disappear under the effects of global warming. Several alpine plants, including snow marguerites cling precariously to life on the edge of such places.

A tramper admires the spring thaw at Ice Lake, South Westland. One of the delights of tramping in the Southern Alps is the almost endless places where solitude and remoteness are in abundance.

Large white flowers of the giant mountain daisy, *Celmisia semicordata*, emerge beside a West Coast stream. Many native New Zealand flowers have simple shapes, and most are white or yellow.

Ski-touring, at the head of the Fox Glacier, with Mts Haast, Lendenfeld and Tasman to the right. Several huts high in Westland/Tai Poutini National Park offer bases for superb climbing and ski-touring trips.

Mitre Peak and Milford Sound, Fiordland National Park. According to Maori legend, the demigod Tu-te-Rakiwhanoa carved all the sounds of Fiordland, beginning in the south and working his way north. By the time he started Milford Sound, the most northerly of the fiords, his skill was such that it became a masterpiece.

Fiordland's Darran Mountains, with Mt Tutoko (2723m) on the left. Due to their notoriously bad weather, climbing on the precipitous granite of the Darran Mountains is a serious undertaking. Trampers can admire the mountains with comparative ease from the Hollyford and Routeburn Tracks.

New Zealand fur seal (*Arctocephalus forsteri*), Martins Bay, Hollyford Track. Previously an important food source for Maori, fur seals were hunted nearly to extinction during the late 1700s and early 1800s by gangs of sealers from the United States and Australia. Since then they have recovered slowly, with their most important breeding sites on the West Coast and Fiordland.

The fantail (*Rhipidura fuliginosa*) is one of several common insectivorous native birds. There are similar species in Australia, and the birds are thought to be more recent arrivals to New Zealand than many endemics.

Podocarp forest, Hollyford valley. Podocarps are a group of endemic New Zealand gymnosperms, with the major species including rimu, matai, miro, totara and kahikatea. These forests once clothed much of New Zealand, but due to logging are now rare, especially in lowland areas. The Hollyford Track passes through some impressive lowland podocarp forest remnants.

Fiordland's upper Hollyford River in different moods – in autumn (below) and after a late spring snowfall.

A tramper crosses a footbridge on the Routeburn Track. One of nine Great Walks, the 32 km Routeburn crosses an alpine pass between the Dart and Hollyford valleys, straddling both Mount Aspiring and Fiordland National Parks.

Lake Mackenzie lies on the Fiordland side of the Routeburn Track, and is a classic example of the type of scenery that has made this track world famous. Like many of the Great Walks, the Routeburn is now so popular that booking is required during the peak season of October to April.

Lake Harris, on the Mount Aspiring National Park side of the Routeburn. A quieter
time to walk the track is during autumn or winter, although avalanche conditions can
make the route impossible after heavy snowfalls. Lake Harris is a good example of a
depression carved by glaciers, later filled by melt-water after the ice retreated.

Ruggedy Island at sunset, Rakiura National Park, Stewart Island. New Zealand's most recent national park, Rakiura encompasses most of New Zealand's third largest island, and offers a wealth of wild coastal scenery.

West Ruggedy Beach, Rakiura National Park, Stewart Island. Few places in New Zealand offer tramping in a such a dramatic coastal environment as that on the North-West Circuit of Stewart Island.

Pingao, Big Bay, Fiordland National Park. Pingao is a native sand-binding plant that occurs on dune lands around the coast, although introduced marram grass has reduced its prevalence.

A banded dotterel (*Charadrius bicinctus*) on a nest at Stewart Island. Ground nesting makes such nests very vulnerable to introduced predators, especially stoats and hedgehogs. Banded dotterels live mainly in the South Island, and many migrate back to Australia for the winter.

Dusk at Kinloch, Lake Wakatipu. Lake Wakatipu is New Zealand longest lake (at 84 km) and was carved by glaciation during the last ice age, which ended some 10,000-14,000 years ago. Two of the most popular tramps in Mount Aspiring National Park, the Rees-Dart and Routeburn Tracks, follow valleys at the head of the lake.

Hidden Falls Creek, from Park Pass, with the Darran Mountains in the distance. Park Pass is on the boundary between Mount Aspiring National Park, New Zealand's third largest national park, and Fiordland National Park, New Zealand's largest.

Mt Aspiring (3033m) at dawn, sentinel of Mount Aspiring National Park. New Zealand's only 3000m peak outside of the central Southern Alps, Mt Aspiring is most often climbed by the northwest (left) or southwest (centre) ridges.

Lake Manapouri, Fiordland National Park, became the centre of one of New Zealand's first major environmental battles when developers wanted to raise the level of the lake for hydro-electricity in the 1970s. Eventually, an inventive underground power station was built, saving the lake level. The 67 km Kepler Track, another of the Great Walks, skirts the northeastern shores of the lake. (Photo Darryn Pegram/Black Robin Photography)

One of New Zealand's most distinctive landforms and tourist attractions, Otago's Moeraki boulders were formed some 60 million years ago. Some of the concretions weigh over two tonnes, and many contain fossils of extinct reptiles.

One of the longer and more arduous tramps in Fiordland National Park is the Dusky Track. Beginning from the west arm of Lake Manapouri, the 80 km track crosses a steep pass and traverses thick rainforest to reach Supper Cove at Dusky Sound, the largest of the park's fiords. After retracing the route back to Loch Maree, trampers exit over the gentle tussock tops of the aptly named Pleasant Range to Lake Hauroko.

Ranunculus sericophyllus, Mount Aspiring National Park, Otago. One of many endemic alpine buttercups, this one grows only in the Southern Alps in high, wet, rocky places. Many native New Zealand alpine plants have no close relatives in nearby countries, yet seem to have evolved inexplicably fast during the relatively brief 5 million year history of the Southern Alps. Their origins still pose something of a mystery to botanists.

Trampers in the West Branch of the Hunter River, Otago. The Hunter lies in a remote and little-visited part of conservation estate outside of national or forest parks.

Rock Burn, Mount Aspiring National Park. Drowning in rivers was so common during the days of European settlement it was once dubbed the 'New Zealand death'. Crossing rivers swollen after heavy rain or during summer snowmelt still poses a serious risk to backcountry trampers, although bridges on the more popular tracks allow all-weather access.

Lindis Pass Scenic Reserve, an exquisite area of high country tussocklands through which State Highway 8 passes en route to Wanaka from the Mackenzie Country. Extensive areas of the South Island are covered in tussock, a type of native grass, but burning, sheep grazing and weed invasion have damaged many such landscapes.

Lake Pukaki, with a distant Aoraki/Mt Cook. (Photo Steve Baker/Black Robin Photography)

Mt Sefton (left) rises as a sharp angular wedge in Aoraki/Mount Cook National Park. This view is from the Upper Hooker Valley, where Empress Hut (above) – one of 17 huts in the park – forms a base for climbers. Many come to try the difficult ice routes on the south face of Mt Hicks, visible behind the hut.

Sunrise on Aoraki/Mt Cook (3754m), from above the Grand Plateau, showing the East Face on the left. During 1991, its height was reduced by some 20m when a massive rock avalanche peeled off the top of the mountain and thundered down into the nearby Tasman Valley. Such events are not uncommon and dramatically illustrate the inherent instability of New Zealand mountains.

The Malte Brun Range lies across the Tasman Glacier opposite Aoraki/Mt Cook. Lines of heavily faulted rock are obvious here, typical of the loose rock that New Zealand climbers have to contend with.

The diminutive rock wren (*Xenicus gilviventris*) is New Zealand's only truly alpine bird. These very rare birds belong to the wren family and eke out an existence amongst rocks and beneath winter snows. (Photo: Steve Baker/Black Robin Photography)

Rock climbing on 'Escalade' at Banks Peninsula's Castle Rock, near Christchurch. Banks Peninsula has volcanic origins, and remaining basaltic dykes now provide locals with some of the country's best crag climbs.

Winter snowfall over Lewis Pass National Reserve. The Maruia valley, where the popular St James Walkway tramp begins, lies at the centre of the photograph.

Frozen tarn, Lagoon Saddle, Craigieburn Forest Park, Canterbury. One of 19 forest parks in New Zealand, areas like Craigieburn are less well-known than the national parks, but offer abundant opportunities for tramping and climbing.

Mt Cook Lily (*Ranunculus lyallii*), Arthur's Pass National Park. Actually not a lily, but the world's largest buttercup, these showy plants form striking floral displays during late spring and early summer.

Waimakariri River, Arthur's Pass National Park. A number of popular tramping routes begin up the Waimakariri, one of dozens of braided rivers that characterise inland Canterbury. Created in 1929, Arthur's Pass was New Zealand's third national park and the first to be formed because people recognised not just the scenic values, but also its flora and fauna.

Dusky dolphins (*Lagenorhynchus obscurus*), Kaikoura. Although relatively small compared with others of the nine dolphin species inhabiting New Zealand waters, Dusky dolphins are fast swimmers. Along with fur seals, whales and sea birds, they form a major attraction for visitors to Kaikoura, where marine life abounds. (Photo: Tui de Roy)

The Seaward Kaikoura Range from Mount Fyffe during a stormy sunrise. The close proximity of mountains to the sea makes Kaikoura one of the most scenic coastlines in New Zealand.

Sawcut Gorge is a unique limestone slot, tucked away in Isolated Hill Scenic Reserve, south of Blenheim. While some 50 metres long and 12 metres high, the gorge is nowhere more than three metres wide.

Mamaku tree fern, Bay of Many Coves, Marlborough Sounds. Visitors to New Zealand often comment on the abundance and size of the ferns. Some, like this mamaku, can reach up to twenty metres high.

Walkers enjoy a quiet moment at Te Pukatea Bay, Abel Tasman National Park. With its golden sands, granite headlands and convivial climate, the coastal walk around this park is immensely popular. Established in 1942, on the 300th anniversary of Dutchman Abel Tasman's arrival in New Zealand, this national park is New Zealand's smallest.

Yacht, Bay of Many Coves, Queen Charlotte Sound. The Marlborough Sounds were formed after rising sea levels drowned several river valleys. Sea kayaking and yachting are favourite activities in the area, as well as mountain biking and walking the 67 km Queen Charlotte Track. (Photo: Darryn Pegram/Black Robin Photography)

Sea kayakers at Medlands Beach, Abel Tasman National Park. Until about ten years ago, sea kayaks were uncommon in New Zealand, but now they are an increasingly popular way to explore the coastlines of places like Abel Tasman and the Marlborough Sounds.

D'Urville Jetty, Lake Rotoroa, Nelson Lakes National Park. Nelson Lakes offers the perfect introduction to Southern Alps tramping. The mountains here are gentler than those further south, yet still have a distinctive glacier-carved shape, and one of the best networks of huts and tracks in any park.

The East Matakitaki valley is one of the lesser-known parts of Nelson Lakes National Park. In the distance are the Spenser Mountains, named by Irish explorer William Travers, who admired the poems of Englishman Edmund Spenser.

South Island robin (*Petroica australis australis*), a sub-species of one of New Zealand's two robin species. Perhaps the most friendly of our native birds, robins will frequently investigate trampers resting on the track, and may even hop onto their boot. Although the South Island robin is not endangered, introduced rats devastate their nests, and the birds are not as common as they once were.

Beech forest above a misty Lake Rotoiti, Nelson Lakes National Park. The area is well-known for its delightful stands of beech forest.

Mountain neinei, Kahurangi National Park. Sometimes forming dense groves, this unusual plant is a giant heath plant endemic to New Zealand, and is often likened to trees in a Dr Seuss book.

Granite blocks above Lake Clara, Lead Hills, Kahurangi National Park. At 452,000 ha, Kahurangi is New Zealand's second largest national park and our most geologically diverse.

Mt Arthur and The Twins from the Tablelands, Kahurangi National Park. The Tablelands, along with other areas of Kahurangi, including the Garibaldi and the Thousand Acres Plateau, were formed in ancient seas and uplifted in more recent times. Beneath the marble of Mt Arthur is the Nettlebed cave system, New Zealand's deepest.

Dawn over Cattle Ridge, Tararua Forest Park. In 1954 the Tararua Ranges became the first forest park in New Zealand. A favourite haunt of Wellington trampers, the Tararuas are well known for their terrible weather. Referring to the often trying experience of battling wind in near-zero visibility, mountaineer and writer John Pascoe once likened them to oatmeal, calling them "Dull, solid fare which gives [you] staple virtues."

Kapiti Island, off the coast north of Wellington. In 1897 the island became New Zealand's third nature reserve, and this predator-free sanctuary is now accessible to visitors as a day trip.

One of more common native birds, tui (*Prosthemadera novaeseelandiae*) were often referred to as the 'Parson Bird', because of the white tuft of feathers under their chins. Tui have an exquisite song.

A bush parrot, the North Island kaka (*Nestor meridionalis septentrionalis*), is now rare in many parts of mainland New Zealand, though still a common sight on Kapiti Island.

Gnarled silver beech forest, near the bush edge on the Tararua Range. High rainfall means the beech trunks are often thickly covered in lichens and mosses.

Early morning light captures tussock tops on the Whanahuia Range, Ruahine Forest Park, Manawatu.

Takahe (*Porphyrio mantelli*), Mana Island, Wellington. Takahe, an extremely ancient and rare native rail, were thought extinct by 1898, but were rediscovered in Fiordland's Murchison Mountains in 1948. Now many breeding pairs have been located to several offshore islands, including Mana and Kapiti.

The Putangirua Pinnacles, one of the Wairarapa's most distinctive
landforms, and an example of 'badlands' style erosion.

Cape Kidnappers, Hawke's Bay's premiere wildlife site. Australasian gannets (*Morus serrator*) were first recorded here in 1870 and now nest in three separate colonies. Captain James Cook named the cape after an incident when local Maori attempted to kidnap a Tahitian boy on board his ship, the *Endeavour*, in 1769.

A stand of kahikatea, New Zealand's tallest tree, at Arahaki Lagoon, Whirinaki Forest Park. This was the last forest park created by the New Zealand Forest Service before the Department of Conservation was formed in 1987.

Red-crowned parakeets (*Cyanoramphus novaezeelandiae*) are one of three species of parakeet, or kakariki, known on mainland New Zealand. The yellow-crowned is the most abundant, with the red-crowned less common, and the newly described orange-fronted parakeet extremely rare. The latter occurs only in North Canterbury, where there are only an estimated 200-500 birds.

The pohutukawa is a coastal tree that produces brilliant displays of red flowers around December, earning it the nickname of the New Zealand Christmas tree. (Photo: Steve Baker/Black Robin Photography)

Dawn cloud over Lake Waikaremoana, as seen from Panekiri Bluff. Created by landslide some 2200 years ago, Lake Waikaremoana is the most distinctive and popular feature of Te Urewera National Park. The 46 km Waikaremoana Great Walk circles the southern and western parts of the lake.

Tramper crosses a stream, upper Tauranga River. Remote bush-clad ranges form the vast majority of Te Urewera National Park, offering challenging tramping.

The common green gecko (*Naultinus elegans*) occurs in forest and scrub areas of the North Island. New Zealand's gecko species are unusual in that all produce live young, a rarity among lizards.

Korokoro Falls (left) is one of many attractive falls in Te Urewera National Park

The kiwi (*Apteryx* spp) is one of New Zealand's ancient endemics and, even though it is the national icon, is in serious danger of extinction on the mainland. Habitat loss, as well as stoat predation on chicks, has been the major cause of decline. Trampers are most likely to see wild kiwi on Stewart Island, where the absence of stoats ensures the birds are present in relatively high numbers. (Photo: Tui de Roy)

Red beech forest, Kaipo River, Kaimanawa Forest Park. The Kaimanawa Range is part of the North Island mountain axis, which also includes the Kaweka, Ruahine, Tararua and Te Urewera Ranges.

North Island kokako (*Callaeas cinerea wilsoni*) is one of three species of endemic wattlebirds. While kokako are still present in several North Island forests, including Pureora Forest Park, Mapara Wildlife Reserve and Te Urewera National Park, the other two species of wattlebird – saddlebacks and huia – have not fared so well. Saddlebacks are now restricted to offshore islands, and the last of the huia became extinct in the early 1900s.

North Island robin (*Petroica australis longipes*), or toutoutwai, Pureora Forest Park. Intensive predator control work in Pureora Forest Park is ensuring birds like the kokako and robin have a future on mainland New Zealand.

Sea kayaking, Western Bays, Lake Taupo. One of the world's largest caldera lakes, Taupo was formed by as series of explosive volcanic eruptions, the last of which occurred in 186 AD and spewed so much ash into the world's atmosphere that both the Romans and Chinese recorded the event.

Dawn, Waihaha Bay, Lake Taupo. New Zealand's largest lake, Taupo is popular for sailing, trout fishing and boating.

Mt Ngauruhoe, Tongariro National Park. The area's stark volcanic landscapes are some of New Zealand most popular attractions. The 37 km long Tongariro Northern Circuit passes Red Crater (centre) before continuing on past Blue Lake (foreground). Mt Ruapehu (visible behind Ngauruhoe) last erupted in 1995 and 1996.

Champagne Pool, Waiotapu, Rotorua. This lake is one of several geothermal attractions in the central North Island. Others include Orakeikorako, Waimangu and Whakarewarewa.

Waipakihi Valley, Kaimanawa Forest Park. Although undoubtedly over-shadowed by the neighbouring peaks of Tongariro National Park, the Kaimanawa Range offers great tramping, deer hunting and fly-fishing.

Emerald Lakes, Tongariro National Park, with the Kaimanawa mountains in the distance.

The distant mountains of Tongariro National Park rise above cloud, as seen from Fantham's Peak on Mt Taranaki, Egmont National Park. Maori legend has it that Mt Taranaki and Mt Tongariro were once side by side and fought for the love of another nearby peak, the maiden Pihanga. Their fight was long and bitter, with Taranaki the eventual loser. He fled towards the ocean, carving the path of the Whanganui River on his way, and still mourns the loss of his beloved Pihanga. Clouds wrapping the summit are said to be his tears.

Syme Hut is the highest hut on Mt Taranaki, perched on the shoulder cone of Fantham's Peak.

Mt Taranaki and the Ahukawakawa swamp from the Pouakai Range. Taranaki is New Zealand's deadliest mountain, with more than 60 climbers having met their deaths on its slopes. Lured by the mountain's accessibility, many would-be climbers underestimate how rapidly the weather can change and how treacherous ice conditions can become.

The Waitotara River, inland from Wanganui, passes through the second largest unbroken extent of forest remaining in the North Island.

Canadian canoeing on New Zealand's most navigable river, the Whanganui. Beginning near Taumarunui in the centre of the North Island, canoeists paddle down some 145 kilometres of the river to finally emerge at the village of Pipiriki. There are dozens of rapids, though none that can't be tackled by relatively inexperienced paddlers. (Photo: Darryn Pegram/Black Robin Photography)

Terereohaupo Falls, on the Waitotara River. Much of the area through which both the Waitotara and Whanganui Rivers flow is an old papa peneplain, formed in ancient seas and since uplifted to its present height.

Waitete Beach, Coromandel Peninsula. Although beaches are what most people come to the Coromandel for, there are walking tracks through bush in the local ranges. Mt Moehau, the highest peak in Coromandel Forest Park, is visible in the far distance.

Hole in the Rock, part of the complex coastline of Northland's Bay of Islands.

Pohutukawa, Fantail Bay, Coromandel Peninsula. Pohutukawa arch over many camping areas around the Coromandel coast, offering welcome shade in the summer.

Tuatara, one of two species of *Sphenodon*, an ancient endemic reptile that dates back beyond the dinosaur era. Tuatara are now extinct on the mainland, but occur on many offshore islands around Northland, the Coromandel and Cook Strait.

Wairere Falls, Kaimai Ranges. Straddling a range dividing the Bay of Plenty from the Waikato, Kaimai-Mamaku Forest Park is one of the lesser-known forest parks.

A kauri tree in Northland's Trounson Kauri Park. Early European settlers were staggered by both the size and straightness of kauri trees, the largest of which were recorded with 20m girths. They didn't lose much time before decimating the kauri forests of Great Barrier, Northland, Auckland and the Coromandel for timber. The largest tree still in existence is Tane Mahutu, which boasts a 13.8m girth.

Pohutukawa and Goat Island, Leigh, Auckland. In 1975 New Zealand's first marine reserve was established here between Cape Rodney and Okakari Point. Since then numbers of fish such as snapper, and crustaceans such as crayfish, have sky-rocketed, and Goat Island is now one of the most popular dive sites in New Zealand.

Flock of oystercatchers, Miranda, Firth of Thames. New Zealand is a vitally important place for migratory shore birds, many thousands of which fly from places as far away as Siberia and Alaska to breed here in the summer.

The volcanic topography of Great Barrier Island, as seen from Mt Hobson. Great Barrier Island, located east of Auckland in the Hauraki Gulf, is New Zealand's largest island free of possums and stoats. Rare birds including kaka thrive on the island.

Ninety Mile Beach. Sand dunes form a major part of the landscapes of Northland's northern tip. Although not actually ninety miles long, this beach sweeps for many kilometres beside the Tasman Sea and, in places, the sand dunes push some one to two kilometres inland. (Photo: Craig Potton)

Subtropical forest containing puriri, nikau, tree ferns and regenerating kauri cloak much of the Waitakere Ranges, near Auckland. A vitally important outdoor playground for Aucklanders, the Waitakeres are one of a series of regional parks around the country managed by local councils, not by the Department of Conservation.

Acknowledgments

Thanks to the support and inspiration of the 'Wellington Freelancers': Dave Hansford, Marieke Hilhorst, Kathy and John Ombler, Dave Chowdhury, Naomi O'Connor, Andy Reisinger, Veronika Meduna and my partner Tania Stanton.

Photography and text: Shaun Barnett

Published in 2001 by Craig Potton Publishing
98 Vickerman Street, PO Box 555, Nelson, New Zealand

Reprinted in 2005

© Photography and text: Shaun Barnett
© Craig Potton Publishing

Printed by Printlink Ltd, Wellington

ISBN 0-908802-80-3